THE
NORTH
WELL

THE
NORTH
WELL

New Poems by

LOUIS COXE

David R. Godine · Publisher · Boston

First edition published in 1985 by
David R. Godine, Publisher, Inc.
306 Dartmouth Street
Boston, Massachusetts 02116

Library of Congress Cataloging in Publication Data
Coxe, Louis Osborne, 1918–
The north well.
I. Title.
PS3505.09637N6   1985   811'.54   84-48752
ISBN 0-87923-566-7

First edition

Printed in the United States of America

Contents

For Bob and Gro and Olav
Lou and Charlie and Helen
with love

THE
NORTH
WELL

Halcyon Days

Does this mean knowledge that I keep alone,
that strikes slant, makes its peace, then goes?
Oh, traces, a wake, providence of things done
and seen. Remember? Who else cares or knows?

Nothing can work for nothing out of a rotting past
that lies by memory cratered like a moon.
Go slow: once easy did it, a cast
arcing in space and angling for more than man.

I could have talked with Einstein, mornings, by Fine Hall,
rapt in his curved equation for the sun
and its outriders. That was before the fall,
that death in Eden where the war got won.

Garden State

Hauling eastward, rainsqualls after dark
tangle and bridge the Hudson at Tappan Zee
where the cars charged with home or distance arc
a bright weld walking water across the bay:
they hiss a flare-path, mass with moment armed
and steady, hurling to their separate wills:
the river under them shifts, they have been warned,
and slides to the city and sea between these hills.
No one moved so can feel the lines of force
that nature charges surging the long way home,
starting nowhere she moves out, or worse
homes-in on man her hunter stocked like game

Nuclear Vessel

The turbines lie still in their housings, the reduction gears
to the twin shafts unturning show no signs
though we can hear the coarse roar of diesel generators
above the air conditioning and the piped pop tunes.
Wide-screen glass bends over the instrument panel,
white men loll by a table of glow and gleam
and wait for a real presence tuning in the channel
where Being flares to the full color of seem
for beyond that bulkhead in its leaden cell
the heart of the matter, the reactor pile,
will rot in fury turning shaft and wheel
alive and kicking as a living soul

Nice Places to Visit

Wing-walking over Iowa all summer,
diving off Castine where the brig went down:
buccaneer's gold shines somewhere under Oak Island
before the fall. It takes all winter to catch cold.

Wing and water draw circles around each other,
go by like targets flying to make up space
where we wait between them, holding patterns
for stow-and-castaway, rumors, hiding places

and you could live there, holding—low, high
between wreckages, sights, sounds
walking around under water, wrung dry
over Aldebaran sometime where it ends

Auden

Fame ran with you all the way from the beginning:
at the end, front pages. Out of breath
last in Austria, still running,
you find what you believed, a second growth.

Your head made a relief map of the moral wars
packed in with wicked fun, disasters, gnomes.
Now enter the kingdom: that's MacNeice
on the stairs to meet you, put you at your ease.

Know that when you enter the best will stand up:
it's a public school there, you get what you earned
the Head's whole justice. You had seen the cup
in a glass darkly. It will fit your hand.

Deathwatch

We speak ill of the dead
to say they live too dark
overcrept where the grave
burying beetle works.

Say they hold their fire
going up over our heads
or swimming circles around
under poles, parallels.

Where they are not is now,
though our breath might give them air
open mouthed like bells,
enough to call them down.

Ezra Pound
ODE FOR HIS TOMB

It was all given me,
first death and last, all one:
Helen, not Penelope
drew me away alone

out of that great war that killing friends
hurt me where I grew:
no war ever ends. Who finds
time in his hands makes all things new

but not in Hell nor out of it, only
myself that utmost isle
perfect alone on Circe's ocean
where nothing grows to fail.

I called it by my name, left home,
kept nothing on this hand
stretched to the sailed sea one way,
on the other, sand

Beacon

Spirit, third eye, refracting glass,
how do you read me—out of flight
and cold wearing attitude for dress
apogee for height and weight?

Planted in dust I came up roses,
nothing puts down my burst of bloom.
Can I go backstairs where man disposes,
knock down my mockup and make room?

Spirit whose laser touch can kill
or heal my vision with a scar,
break from the orbit of your will
and fill me to bursting like a star.

Country Matters

The river's renal yellow
traffic reaming home
dead set in its silo
minuteman

Limbs like shadows on air
sycamores writhe
Ginkgo and ailanthus thrive
by their own rancor

Only the fit few
exchanging cold for heat
flash their wakes on the night
to keep the course true

Light After Dark

Show me how the hills move
in shadow, how the sea
signs, islands peak and pine:
I'll believe you: believe me.

What have I done to you these years?
Love's no dark miracle: it makes its own
marvels by daylight. Let desires
move their mountains. Love alone
stands still under shadow, stays home—

no, not for death, too long life even,
but for the believing heart, God's gift
to the ungifted who must try
to learn how harm's the way love left
and must come back by.

Sense of an Ending

The locust rasps August
a burr of sun
fretting the season's edge.
Now's the way to live now
to keep time
clear but out of haze
to go together
but strange.
In each spurt of heart
a season speaks
and nothing changes we call change
only it moves, goes dark.
I speak
you speak to me, I never heard
It was the locust at his sound
I listened to waiting for it to end

Crazy Sunday
(SCOTT FITZGERALD AND OTHERS)

Sundays they build character in the wild weather
of Buffalo and Green Bay or where St. Paul
and Minneapolis cross the river and flow together
to freeze three hours into some kind of ball—

not that game of hearts Fitzgerald dreamed
pining after Hobey Baker in the shade
of his own goalposts, blonder even than Yale . . .
too slight to play now, in shadow and damned.

Every day is Monday morning, the games all tied
Fitzgerald wakes to, played over and over, hard rock
and porn. It was in France in '17 they all died
the heroes, poets and peasants. All that lot

who woke to weather in their rotten fields,
lightning in the sky, or early snow.
No current moves. Frozen before he falls
last Sunday's hero finds a way to go.

Mobile Home

Days shrink empty going fast:
it's never light enough or warm.
Even when ball games smear the tube well after dark
the world keeps turning young—

they swarm all over frightful in hair
and rags like a rabble army in discharge.
His own enemy—old, half in despair,
sick with world, with zeals like lost baggage.

The California children phone
high holidays and the secular feasts
but can't write. He lets it ring long
sometimes. Too many pasts.

Equal Time

The way out and the way in,
the wrong way up and down,
dance the planets so they say:
enough? too much. Get out.
Wake. Get even. Watch the day
rotten at morning, dead by four
nourishing sky, out to get
the watcher fixing on his star.

Cold. Does weather keep the world
or the world its weather? For a time
we had those rockets, capsules, men
shot on target, beating the field
to catch all the prizes. That was then.

Let it go. Do you wonder how weather
can keep us going? In their pools
the spent rods fester. Now or never
will the sills rot, the paint peel.
Tax time. Shall I pay again
for my system broken down, on screen?
Stars will shatter and still burn,
wonders take over, turn and shine.
All yours and mine.

Sunday Drivers, Marblehead

Over the causeway where the big autumn blow
scooped and battered, townies and tourists wheel
in funeral. Wreckage—white on blue
bursts upward, flumes along the wall.

A latter spring? No, familiar fall
with its moral sermon ready to sound and fade
over and over. In the midst of love
we are in debt. No man ever gave
a dime to oblivion just to play the fool.

Wakes on water, jet trails, a torn road
around a sudden boulder: all these sign
a way someone will travel. Stripes across a field
or a sky form particles, crystals, positions held:
against all odds we run here for the ride.

The A Train

How long, how late, never to know
thinking forever on the wrong side of the head,
everything slides, forever stops now
give or take these years. Bring out your dead.

"The world's not such a bad old bugger"
even Beckett says. I can go along.
Seeing and hearing through filters, stumble to stagger,
everyone gets to somewhere. Memory Lane?

I like that old tune, that flat blare
the Ellington sound, how his black arts
twisted the straight and turned an outside in
where the few who follow can break out where it hurts.

Flight Number

At your age I went to war—
you might have gone—
ran away is more
the way I went, alone.

I can feel you going now
seas over in flight
after some girl you know
or maybe knew, you thought.

What dream of lose or win
drives or leads you there
wherever it is you run
overseas, on air?

Native

He cranks, hermetic in his stink,
his insult through the summer places
watching the owners twist and shrink
inside as if he held their noses.

He pushes blackberries. The bribe passes
with its indulgence palm to palm:
making his fortune owners' business
he hangs fire like gun.

Charged with fear and outland anger
cringed to an attitude, he waits
upwind, obsequious and longer:
he comes and goes by what he hates.

Ruin of body, name and nature
caught in the failing light take glare
like rot in heartwood, on pond and pasture,
all that he owned once on fire.

Constellation

Brimful of horizon trees the north well
tips out stars, great winter bear
skinned, nailed to the north wall,
and I watch that slide screened inside my head.
No one goes out there, ever—never will,
never the same space we drift in twice.
Feet apart upright pinned to the ground
I watch stars stream out from a well—
dead souls of explorers racing for the pole.

Gone South for the Winter

Whichever wind blunders around this house
north keeps the name that changes going west
like the planets shifting. Venus loose
over horizon ranges and slips past.

Lakes like Erie reek under the winter lid
spring may lift again—may not, depending.
Who would depend on tilt, slide, upending
this incontinent land shifting its load
to the southern shoulders above and below the line?
Natural shellbacks following the sun
we take the loot, run and go it alone
leaving the old place to heave or hold it down.
Warm down here. Friendly. We like it fine.

Miracle

You gave me sight. It doesn't work
the way you told me. After dark
where no one can follow me around
a touch will bond me head to hand
shade to shadow, drawing blind
down to nothing. I saw trees
walking like men. Where did they go?
You lied to me: sight is what you see
but I saw visions and I know

Building the Ark

Will the god who set that flood
last time, this time set fire?
Sensors and angels seeking heat
climb to surrender. What was star
crumples inward cold and dense
as a presidium, trails a trace
of moral meaning, a new tense
out of its elements, a whole new race.

Daughters and sons, true friends and killers,
listen: it is your prophet speaks:
tear it down. No creeps, no crawlers
this time with blessing in their beaks.

Litany

As I slump down from middle age
keep me I pray from hate and rage,
from torture of eye and ear and mind,
keep me safe or stone me blind
with staring at the wrinkled map
of a model world the times blew up.

"Awake my soul, stretch every nerve":
keep me from passing on the curve
lest on the wrongside road I meet
strangers and brothers in defeat.
To pestilence of human spawn
make me indifferent as a moon
that chaste and cratered has no mind
to line up with a sun gone blind.

In flame and blackness keep me whole,
caulk the fissures of my soul
with hardening doubts that seal together
my separate parts, keeping out weather:
cut out rot, patch me new,
measure and plane me to fit true.

Lastly, that I may know mine end,
teach me how to reach my friends
my wife my children that they in turn
reaching me neither freeze nor burn,
know who's there, see him move
cursed and blest like them in love,
dying before their eyes as they
loom and enchant and fade away.

Now in the soul I pray survives
find faith that touches all our lives.
Hear me! before the fiend bursts out

to mock me up a TV tout,
give me long views or short, no more
garden or desert, sea or shore

Pulsars Are People

Each weighs ten tons at least, wringing wet
but with solid fire perhaps where they swim,
stellamorphic dream their element
riding their pulses down.

Several lifetimes of light years make their moment
whirling in a second what we spin a long day:
we might pass them over O'Hare or Logan
and neither signal nor sign. Neither would they.

Let their quick pulses race palping our dying planet,
we can hear Doppler-effect groaning as they move near
then away again, as some animal might vanish
whose sensors signalled we would open fire.

In the Beginning

My drive-in banker runs out cold
under my overdraft. No Arab crude.
I'll mine my money, my fool's gold
in the one vein left me: this old trade.

Words to bring home, tend their wounds
and let them go again hale, healed
of the hurt that ailed them, no more afraid
of the mouthing that fouled them than of change.
Because they live by what I say
as I by what they sound. No wonder
greater than that. What can I pay
more than they give me going under?

Convert

I ate what was put before me
after the fashion. Who now knows
how the diet sets? The old toad
dies daily for my meat.

God's creed blood and body
I swallowed. When I throw them up
they clog my gorge. Bloody
begun, bloody ended. Pass the cup.

A Room of Her Own

She writes pretty letters to her daughter
about how neat the nurse is, how her window
widening over lawn winnows light and water
in the fall rains. All suffering's divorce.

Winter. She writes verses, feels more
no better. The words break out
like boils as the days turn in out of sure
despair sundered from cause: her first doll,
the girl she writes to. Daddy humbled all
her plays and players. No there out there.

Beyond pity for herself or a season
dripping with changes she will trail her grief
over her child's threshold, being chosen
to return calls on the world, to charge a life.

EKG

That's a heartbeat that the stylus scribes:
terra incognita. The few who've landed there
may get where they're going while the country thrives.
Questionable, right now: it's no unbounded sphere
but the real thing making up lies
as it goes along. The small print leaps and jags
like radar blips, sonar. It's wild country
out where that red pump flaps like a paper bag
and the electrodes keep their counsel in peaks and pinnacles
as the current rushes its message through
what might have been gentle country, a good place to visit
but blundered and bruised too long now. Nothing new.

Dark Sister

This child of chance takes the night air
live in the vapor lamp's morgue glow.
Can she feel that stare
bent from the scope on her
in shape darker than shadow?

Shot siren bullhorn or tire squeal:
something is out this late
after some dark other turning pale,
out perhaps of sight:
most vision is white.

Whoever speaks her she'll lead home:
they will take hands, those two
under the cold vapor before dawn
saying yes or now
and going one by one

Phaethon

The will I was born with and the now wave,
pressure against cells, this vessel's skin:
I watch my own arts cast themselves a scene
I saw: I teach myself to drive.

Now I can make me up, go on striking
styles, altitudes, lines, a whole new vein
to work out nights or shoot as white as lightning:
it's the second not the first leap makes gain
where I can leave my desert bones to whiten
out in the blue away from all that green.

Aphasia

It never came on time
to reach me, the late news:
my dates were wrong, the beam
swept out but didn't scan.

Out there blip and beep
came on ticking the time
to others. Caught in the sweep
I turned them out of tune

into shapes of plot and pattern
that leapt on the scope and died
telling me "No matter."
Whatever I did, they lied

to me alone. This sickness
fingered and fed with dark
stands as sole witness
to a long night's work.

Learning to Read

Something from memory, for life
and nothing but words. What else is new?
Images burn at the back of the brain,
a knife in wood. The past is now.

There's more there than you can know or name
but listen: implausible life, wild fires
burn like a bush God keeps alive:
martyrs, fools of fortune rave
or speak by silences. Listen. Love.

Better than living? Worse? Books live
by opening out. They never end
but closed like flowers under the sun
they reach, they open, they take love
from language, the spirit that made man.

August waits too long for its latter rain
and the sense of an ending. No more green
to keep the world real. Winter works with stars
to get along with. Only sinking flares.

There should be charts showing the track we came
intricate out of origin—now simpler grown.
Our sky still scatters, its swimmers rowing home:
what ways they go with all our time to burn.

Right to an answer? Wait for the question. Who
told us to take our time? Who broke our case?
We know the ways around: go in, get through
where senses are endings and kingdoms keep their keys.

Euripides' Helen

I never went to Troy: that was a ghost
living from my dead body. An unknown queen
in Sparta, where the boys are, I made most
of what was given me, the flip side of the coin.

I would have loved those wars. Sparta's closed down
twelve hours a day all the round year,
nothing but sex to do. When the boys are gone
off playing jock it's sad country for a queer

but I can't—never could—do it all the time:
better to burn down Troy a living ghost
and haunt the future. True beauty's a crime
all of us pay for with our peck of dust

Gawaine and The Green Knight

Take my hand. Rise and walk carrying
your own head by the hair.
Do you hear angels on antenna-tips,
along waves and wires? They keep the air
and flame like corposants. You can tell
these several passing splendors make the deadly sins
who come when you call.
Speak to me. Tell me time. Whose head
staring the way I go turns in my hands
but will say nothing? Set it there—so.
Now. Speak from these shoulders. I have raised the dead.

Horrible Parable

Once these towns were textile, part of the parish
that wore fortunes out, the migrants down.
Now look: past renewal pornhouses even the Irish
decline like Yankees, a day's march nearer home.

Will the great quake come out of Africa? Boyars flourish
under the particulate dome? Will all the generals howl
at a probe of middle air, crying on courage
of cruises, back fires, the penultimate cloud . . .
who promised the ending from the start—tall tales
of gardens, snakes and fire? We all know,
or used to, that old gardener whose tools
broke the ground open, made Now
out of a yesterday he had no mind
for knowing, remembering nothing, stoned blind.

Nightsong

Just as a year might end
the world tonight may die
around the darkside moon
with one wipe of the eye.
The world makes something to see
if we go out and look
at fields of snow and stars:
the ogle eye of Mars
throbbing toc and tic
burns red in the dark.
See how it all ends,
this time that was never ready,
this future that never worked
fallen into our hands
and our hands deadly
and the dead, friends.

Midwatch, Leaving Christmas Island

We went out alone, searchlight breaking dark:
dazzled, fish flew to the wing of the bridge
and broke. As the ship blacked out
war set us like a watch.

I go back to my old city, the merchant trader
where Hawthorne darkened, Bowditch set his stars
in a navigable heaven of uneven fires,
Jones Very dreamed of angels on their ladder:

coming or going? In an acre of back yards
like Blake I saw angels in a Seckel pear,
a brier burning, evenings drawing down
and war afire in the west. I went there

Getting-up Morning

Who moved the stone
Not I legion said
I quit when I'm ahead
You can't make it alone

Who unbound the corpse
Not I mother said
My son is dead
Nothing you say helps

Who was at the door
Not me I said
I was home in bed
This may mean war

East of the Sun

Late summer west of the moon they start their burn
coming down for air.
Orion totters, Venus slips water-borne
What matters is fire
the shudder as the weather-breeding plumes
of cirrus cusp and trail
east of a dead sun where horizon gathers
dark, and they hold the fire they feel
as though day might never come again.
Knowing it will come they keep still
in the quarter where weather breeds with time
till they all fire at will

Laureate

Another wake to follow
on less than a dollar a day:
I hear good things to say
about it. My own folly
born with me rings
around me. Go away . . .

What has the god given
that I can make good?
only a lifelong knack
starting over and even . . .
make him take it back:
received. Not understood.

Intersection

One more morning waiting out the light.
What do the signs say?
"No. You turn. Dead end. Keep right.
That life. This truth. No way."

Homing on dark the armed and armored beasts
close in breathing behind you foul mouthed.
Speed spoils first, then kills, rests
at the red and amber, mass and moment clothed.

Think of China up against that wall
keeping the hordes out who let devils in
to the sacred, the hidden, the enabling will
that forces time. Can evil never win?

Only as tide turns. That king who called
water to stand knew men came from the sea
his empire. Water holds up the world
and will take it back, so all the angels say.

Loyalist Song

Our founding fathers sleep:
they might have known. We knew
dreams are for making up,
only the real comes true.

Offscourings, peasant scum
upstarting against their betters
make themselves at home
believing whatever happens.

Hear how their freedom rings.
What else can it do?
Fit only to kill kings
as if that made it new

Another Country

In the long dead of night when heat
falters between two elements, under the dial
that points to dawn and back again,
gnomon of dark waiting for sun and time,
the house ticks and crackles like fall ground.
A wind winds around out of ocean, east to west
hauling snow from sea and letting go.

    The algorist of six o'clock
    hearing the radiators knock
    like valves of the heart, must pray for sun
    and wait for the coffee to get done.

    There's sea-smoke under a failed moon,
    the dog fox lifts his head. Not one
    fouled river reeks or grinds
    under the ice it works and winds

    Where this winter comes and goes
    only a mathematic knows
    curving a möbius band from sleep
    and back again, with time to keep.

    I once knew one who wove all winter
    spells of ice that locked his rage
    in the heart of a glacier, lion country
    once, now careful as a cage.

Mechanic

Grew up before they changed the rules
leaving him sucking foul air.
Now he notices: the tools
they gave him to stroke the circle square
were trophies of the bend and torque
that ground him to an end they willed:
back on his hands now, out of work,
something's gone wrong that wants his skill.

Outside at play like blowing grass
the others, free to live forever
and keeping young, blare like brass
the tenor that can blow his cover.
Who's he now, now he knows
nothing and needs it to wind it back,
take it apart and find the use
and good it keeps, make it spark
as though time, trod like a tire
and running forever in line and true
full pressure without heat or wear
might run him home before it blew.

Home

Look out there where the window ends
in blinds and shade: the shadow runs
away to woods growing awry
in run-out pasture. Why not try
the overhead that clamps a lid
on zero ground, the outer edge
of upward where there might be open
space to load with common human.

This may be the day: can you tell time
just checking pressure, your upper arm?
Flights of angels, codes, mixed bags
all taking to strangers. Will they take back?
Change arcs inward, time implodes
to denser silences gone cold
here in the heart that fibrillates and chatters
alone, not caring used to it, mutters
into the voice-tube its vital signs.
The weather promises. Everything ends.

Not out there: look through the pane
projecting billions, figures far
and away but always heading home.
Where is it? when? what's it for,
not what it is or can be ever:
it's an end, a window, even a heaven
open to enter, to say grace
to the lucky who land there and know their place

The Gift

Let it go down and around again:
how much finer now, and knowing more.
what we remember never coming true
but lovely in growing: is that how we know
the old beauty and its neighbor new
the first time round forever?

Traffic spins away out on the ice—
danger, the signs say
good games for all keeping us young
in hope. Was there a doctor in the house?
The heart, even the head, may learn to keep:
hearts are good keepers given the right room.
I know someone who gave me her heart
and took mine, a gift, the best of me I know

Morning

Morning campfires guttering out,
time to pack it all in flight canoes.
The lifting sun burns inching
higher out of the east. We paddle the freshet run
making ripples out of dawn, drift with the breeze,
puckering shadows spreading over a lover's lake,
heart-shaped pond under shore trees
and water shatters. This is what it says:
     lapping along shore
     tapping a dark green hide
     my lakepond trembles blue kingfisher fire.

Light airs puff the clouds, there shatters the dark,
here splinters of morning, pondy woods,
a gawk heron stilting to a treble breeze
as the paddles trouble the water we calm the airs
keeping the gentlest tenor for such days

Wonder

These are the wonder days alive
after the melt when water rimes
with gutter and sluice. Springs bubble and purl
in the back yard where the kids shoot aggies,
darts on a board. They "dree their weird."

March whistles its oboe noises in the window-jamb.
Why not, alors, then? It's not dumb,
just making the first stab at the last season
never to come back, but tacking up wind.

Nifty and singable the trees thresh
and the kids float sticks, more submarine
than airborne. In the wash of tires
the kids splash. Birches reach for green.

How lovely this dwelling-place. God the host.
Hoping for a trace of wisdom, those three of the tribe
who, struck by a planet's flash, knelt down unsaying
but with a sound to sing. They knew, almost

Geology: the Fraser River

The ache that toils the globe
makes out as nothing does
only on islands or the unsettled streets.
In San Francisco the cable cars may come back again
up and down, tourist traps. The city hangs
like any pinnacle. Nothing made here
but money. Only the poor burrow and hide.

Higher up on the map, Vancouver,
Canada calling. From the high north the Fraser River
breaks out and away at last into sea
twisting and battering. It will serve
only its own, whatever this river owns

Wild with mountains, terror-struck, then naked
in prairies, the wind shaking the polar cold.
On the map's high left-hand corner feel the ache
Alaskan. Beyond, the wicked ice thickens
a path to Russia. Panic running.

Cold calm here in Maine, a moose morning
in fall. The great antlered beast, innocent standing,
shudders once after rifle-shot, blood purls,
the big rigs head south with innocent kill.

Old Fraser butts his thick head against walls.
How many broke hearts and fortunes greeding for gold
and the fierce of it. So many, how many died there
held hard in ice, tormented in stream.
Fraser struggles, breaks open into sea

CAPITOLS

Wars grow up here under the dome
unsound and breaking. At heart
a pacemaker ponders going its road.
Inside turns out, the old gut wonders
if the worlds will die when the bowels burst.

Sweet sun in autumn keep shining
even after the last day take heart.
Why should what man grew keep going
after the ending? Raise a new ghost.

A set of cloud ambles over the pane
into another country. They say the bomb
will darken regents, even. Even burn
host and guest at ease, at home
waiting for Godot and the uttering wind.

Light

The weather waves, worlds go on
doing what little they can. There's less
of everything. We've won
most of the wars we've tried.

Outside, fog builds in, uneasy, trying to stay
for whatever reason. Not even hope
to work around. Go search the sky
for missiles screaming without sound
but remembering love even in darkest age
Everything's out there, warning but waving home

Old Glory flips its pole. Swaddled in flags
those good old boys playing their war games flutter
their stripes and stars. A gilt bird, an eagle
tips that pole, wings spread to glory in all weather

How Now

Tinker toy, daddy bike
all the kiddies like a lot
at any age and play with toys
blowing up the other guys

Down the alleys of the heart
gangs turn cold, others burn
working out with nifty bombs
smart as aliens in the corn

Work away. It's half-past-time.
Tools down. There was a duke who broke
a phalanx, scattered troops that burst
riderless. The king who knew
tinkered with a bomb and blew
just to show us who was who.
Only me and you

A la Mode

All that they wanted fell in with the ditch
turning one lover. He had the time,
swung the door open, let both of them roll
down a blueberry bank. Bastard and bitch
lunging together. They had a ball

Came home late, mucked-up car
still working. She rolled another pill
another banger in the sullen air
Let anyone look or laugh. The feel
of what the doctor palped and probed
cleared them, shoved them home.

Mothers and fathers got the news late
not minding much. Each liked both.
All married up, they picked a date,
a peace of justice. Her dress was white.

Time

ONE

May might be that time, this honey taste
crouched on the tongue, lickspittle and fire
for a moment. Outside all green.
The man next door commutes to the hospital
where his wife waits. Both know for what

In oceans, on the comber's crest,
a white spirit startles, curls in foam
slantwise into the sand, spreads out
peeling away back and rowing under.

Sunday. Did someone believe once? Vestiges.
The hospital keeps its secrets. In its halls
the standing ambulation, the coats of white
sign messages. Take to the hills,
look down over the water where the wind
riffles incoming tides, good messages move and send.

TWO

One drink two drinks three drinks five
hardly a lush is now alive
six drinks going down back one
and the feeling's gone

Summer stands. Full tide before retreat.
You and I, all new, come from the sea,
the salt savor smart on the tongue
giving out life, repeat repeat
full flavor on the wing

THREE (The Triple Axe)

In the ungovernable and overgrowing cities and post-cultures
unbelievable unbelieving, head quarters,
the wind from top-and-bottom holes
sends out the message, Ghengis Khan
reborn babbling his flatulence as a killer king
stumbles open-eyed among his sycophants

Who lives a real life under the pall
of the call to arms, hell in the capital cities
and no one to blame but every soul blameworthy?
The householder hanging on to what keeps his peace
hopes it will hold. The dead-reckoners
guess at a course, blessing the keel and the true-coming
dreams. Days rumble past
in armies, bridges blown, hell in and out of the tube,
men women the simple child at growth
turning simpler and silent in a caul of ages.

Well, we can suppose something of that same sort
happened before, hell can hold, chieftains hire halls
for nothing, being mouths on the airwaves,
most of us strangers, our powers darkness,
our prayers to the fetish a dim potency
and under the laws, in the cell-blocks, the dark committees
wring out their terrible languages. The axe comes down

Vines along the bricks
festering the wall that climbs from red to green
would speak if they could
They force perhaps a pattern making gain
as they crawl in their growing across the colors
playing games of hearts.

Telltale silence in leaves
in the sky Blue Angels riot
curving strait as the world
spins, a kind of spirit,
wild devil who weaves
patterns, keeps quiet.
Bright angels strike for home

A single cell will make me whole
that's how it goes
groping for pattern, breaking out
homing-in but wise
enough to keep the peace,
it works, will wait
watching itself alone

Alone. Green peace. The day fails like a heart
searching a past where days keep countenance.
Together as long as it lasts, let it last long
and well, then setting west look east.
The spirit, the real king, strikes the balance

Listen against the grappling of green vines
feeling branch and bark:
the realms of gold, comfortable, not kind
but great places for travel sailing the Ark
from California east to the matter's heart
on a willawaw wind, a people's airline

Hospital corridors rooms for waiting pans
Almost like a populace at home
in capitols and aiming to stay,
fragments of childhood remembered alongshore.
The hospital man, all ruins and shards,
watches, can wait
for his soul to be called home. At the end, he wins.

Hoping wisdom and making work together,
fun for all at the top of the trade.
Funny, in fact, how little the wise men
knew. But they knelt down, they prayed
trying belief   giving. Why?
It was a world out there
still is needing the best
of prayer, but most and last the Word

FOUR (Hide-and-Seek)

Here's hiding again—once more, maybe the last—
in the child's thicket hoping to be found
neither soon nor late   just standing   run down
into memory lies mostly unspoken, but lived.
How? There are ways. It's never the real end.

        Let the rain slake down
        then breaking sky
        let the sun burst
        and the days ponder
        last in line, the rain
        runs after the sun,
        wonder how at first
        it looked around, cast
        from rod and reel
        a strike at last. The god
        his bow bent and steady
        can hold, will make his mark
        then let go

CODA

Call it all in together
make believe
Overhead   inside   outback
green   green

Seasons turn their weather
then squaring away
move nearer, farther
joining the dance, they fly,
blue angels moving nearer
farther than white   white

Is this the honey taste
the grain gold?
A new season laves
south and east
It's a feast of honey
      sun   rain
for the child, the lover
and the wind west

A Touch of Spring

Whatever did the April deed
does it again. Sun's opening eye
traces a carbon track. Wake up
for greed: roll over, make way.

Time is a killer with a gentle touch:
I can feel it palping. Soft days,
older, many scars mostly healed
preach how to live, even to grow
wise almost, a gentler field.

Caissons of cloud dragging the day along
and carrying sometime living rain
into the open to meet sun; the thing
done, or done for, right or wrong
plants April greening again.

Greeting. A Scots April, water
drawn up from earth a god again
to touch the human, a wrung cloud
that gentles, tears of common things

Of Making Books

There's no man's end. You can't put up
or down the telly. Punch it out.
We were hanging on hope, on the Master's breath,
wake up, kick it in the belly
clamp down like teeth.
Haven't a habit except for self
that sweetheart who chuckles cheek and tongue.
Human error? What else
ring-a-peal-a-gong.

There Is One End
will start and find
and plenty kicking outside in.
Kick the right one, that out of date one
Break him like wind

Stroking

He backed against a wailing wall,
rebounding squash ball, tell-tale heart,
and let who took the middle line
stroke for the corner where the ball died.

Winter breeds ice. Puck   stick   check
just short of dirty made his game.
Linesmen let him go. Back home
his fans fell for that dirty work
the summer game. Why should a ball
or a sphere mid-airborne make time and money?
The perfect war-play? work? The wall
can kill it cold. Not many will

Lodgers: Doing Time

Bail's the bottle, jail's the lodge
that fills the hostel where the lodgers keep
and do their time. Each day battles,
most nights black out, some shot through
with terror. How can they get back home?
Can the wedge each border pounds against the walls
of heart and steel fill up sullen time?

The far gone navies, hooker bombs,
swim or sink beginning all over.
Old men will send the young away, the young
believing. Time out. Hymns
quiver open chapels. A saviour
will stride among us, believing
that we believe, warring over again.

Soul is the field, battle the standing ground:
it's only the Other who breaks the nucleus down
tired by waiting, home run where he strikes.
Vessels in Pearl Harbor, middle easts
break and open. Money, unreal.
The old men in their bunkers gnaw like beasts

Grandfather Clause

I think of him riding up from Bangor, going
out of the white cold into the black tunnel.
Salem old city beckons its moving past,
my grandfather's ride, the hunter priest
working for souls with wit and a final saying.

Clear days at Harvard, senior advocate
true wit undergraduate moving at ease
to the vocal pulpit, psalms, the voice I never heard
but sometime found in my echoing head.
Who was that man? I keep his name, almost my own.

Clerics abounding. Families, church mice and souls.
Most never spoke Catholic, but somehow touched
on the stone that settles ground, the peace
that passes understanding and the tunnel, dark
looks for the Light, night-watch and the coming-out.
Going-up or riding the priest still speaks
a laying-on of hands

Jerusalem One (Manahatta)

No friends in office? Spinning the globe
and pondering I wonder who gets to work
happy and honest. The money mill spins away,
sees where it went, how it goes
now, old news made over, spinning down

It's lively and lovely where two seasons
stumble on one another. A small boy
a taller girl circling around
not needing to know, just growing   being.
How   where will they go that's better? Joy
today, tomorrow how. It's those minutes flying
too close over hostile borders, the fleet days
steadying, calm, the hurricane's eye

The best shows this season, namely the past
and today's tomorrow roundabout and reaching.
Close the office doors. Open tomorrow
a working Sunday. Let's move out,
bring home back where it belongs

Two: Jerusalem

Tracking the District, looking for places
other than capitol, towers where nothing's made,
where geek gobbles, guru sits still
What's there to do
around the clock, in their places, a this
aiming to strike that?

The cathedral, tourist bazaar, galleries for fun
fine tower views. Go see the nucleus
swarming the stone that will never burst.
No one lays charges here. We've won
most of our wars. Towers too hardly made
glitter their class act. Closed embassies.
Wars are made here.
How nice to know. Crossing Central Park
in middle dusk, something clenches, danger
in darkness, a fell beauty perhaps? and the pylons blaze,
the avenues turning in, lamps, late walkers
pick up their pace, they know
that light may win. Time works forever

Compass Rose

I waited for the full tide, not the neap
though it has to be taken when you've got to go.
But why? well, reap the harvest, head for the beacon
that blinks its beam. East and west
and round the compass, that's how.

Some kind of Sahara that I aim for
to dry out? Is water dry?
maybe a martini? It's neap tide
by the calendar. Poseidon's drink
pronged on a pitchfork. Will that make wrong
from rote? Listen: I, Tide, speak.

The mini-mountain that looks east
backs against the west. East beckons,
the needle compass prowls between
south and east. There are other points for taking.
I could go any of those wheres
if the fine needle settles in the rose

On Trying to Read Dante
"ME RITROVAI PER UN SELVA OSCURA"

Lost in his woods I can still tell trees
by the look and touch, even the smell:
Overhead, one of our familiar skies
opens or shuts. His world has the feel
of a place I might have come from once before
or might go back to having been long lost
after the last derision of the revolving door
expelled me. Yet here is a deeper forest.

I can see everything stands for something else:
as a child I knew almost everything to know
and now this wise man tells me again himself:
I can believe, almost, dead wood can grow
in perfect effluence, without cause or end,
toward that locus of original sane time ago,
that radical familiar, God's universe as planned.

In those beginnings there is still the Word,
the everyday plods on with bated breath
through spheres of marvel all sleights of the Lord
and I feel a motion toward meaning, something of faith
that can tell men from trees walking by absolute art
married to knowledge faithful unto death
that curves beyond me its unbroken arc

THE NORTH WELL

was set in Weiss by DEKR Corporation, Woburn,
Massachusetts. The book was printed and bound by
Haddon Craftsmen, Scranton, Pennsylvania.
The paper is S.D. Warren's #66 Antique,
an entirely acid-free sheet.

Designed by Anne Chalmers.